Praise and Worship with Flags

Waging Spiritual Warfare in the Church and Home

Delores Hillsman Harris

WestBow
PRESS
A DIVISION OF THOMAS NELSON

WestBow Press books may be ordered through booksellers or by contacting:

WestBow Press
A Division of Thomas Nelson
1663 Liberty Drive
Bloomington, IN 47403
www.westbowpress.com
1-(866) 928-1240

Because of the dynamic nature of the Internet, any web addresses or links contained in this book may have changed since publication and may no longer be valid. The views expressed in this work are solely those of the author and do not necessarily reflect the views of the publisher, and the publisher hereby disclaims any responsibility for them.

Any people depicted in stock imagery provided by Thinkstock are models, and such images are being used for illustrative purposes only.

Certain stock imagery © Thinkstock.

ISBN: 978-1-4497-2766-6 (sc)
ISBN: 978-1-4497-2765-9 (hc)
ISBN: 978-1-4497-2767-3 (e)

Library of Congress Control Number: 2011917375

Printed in the United States of America

WestBow Press rev. date: 11/02/2011

Permissions

About the cover. The dark clouds represent the presence of God or the Lord Jesus. In scripture, 2 Samuel 22:12 (KJV) says, "And he made darkness pavilions round about him, dark waters, and thick clouds of the skies."

The author's website is www.PraiseAndWorshipWithFlags.com.

To those who praise and worship with flags

The Lord is *our* Banner.

Contents

Forward

I am honored to write the forward to this insightful, engaging work on the use of flags in worship. In this day when worship arts has taken its rightful place in our worship experience, Delores has written this book with clarity, practicality and application for pastors and those who want to take worship arts to a new dimension. Her determination to ground her work in scripture is only exceeded by the revelation she shares from the scriptures. Her theology is sound. Her biblical history is on point. All of this is done in a manner that anyone can understand. I so enjoyed the book that I am now going to use it as one of the teaching tools in our Worship Arts Ministry. Up to now, I have enjoyed the ministry of flags during worship. After reading Delores' book, I now understand the purpose and power of flags in worship, and so will you. Finally, Delores takes us beyond our natural senses of enjoying flags in worship. She takes us to the biblical knowledge that flags can heal, deliver and set free in the context of worship. This seminal work is going to cause the kingdom to grow in worshipping and praising our Heavenly Father and it will cause you to grow as well.

Bishop Geoffrey V. Dudley, Sr., D.Min.
Senior Pastor
New Life in Christ Interdenominational Church

Preface

The Holy Spirit intervened visibly in my life on two occasions. First, while I was driving on the Autobahn in Germany, I got lost. I called out to the Holy Spirit, "Help!" Immediately my hands released the steering wheel. The wheel turned on its own, off the highway and onto the exit ramp, from the exit ramp onto a street. I then recognized where I was. My hands were given control of the steering wheel. I was surprised and amazed. I knew that the Holy Spirit had taken control of the car and me.

A second incident showed me the Holy Spirit at work. While taking a shopping trip from Germany to Czechoslovakia, I had been sharing my experiences about the Holy Spirit with my traveling friend. She didn't believe me. On the return from Czechoslovakia to Germany, in the wee hours of the morning on the Autobahn, my friend was driving while I slept. She woke me to point out something that was unclear and questionable in the fog down the highway. I could see taillights. I told her to move the car three lanes over, from the far left lane to the far right lane. I saw her hands on the steering wheel, turning the wheel to the right as we passed the unknown something on the highway. Then we heard loud crashing sounds behind us. We imagined there had been a pile-up of cars as they smashed into one another in the fog. My friend and I looked at each other. I said I was glad she had steered the car off to the right. She said she did not turn the steering wheel. I told her I saw her hands turn the wheel. She said she did not, and I told her the Holy Spirit did it.

Twelve years passed after these two incidents in which the Holy Spirit had provided help and protection from danger. He then makes His presence known again with the flags.

In 2003, while I was in church, praising God and dancing to music with one streamer in my right hand, the streamer—a form of a flag—"took off" on its own. It was no longer under my control. It was in my right hand. I wasn't moving it or directing its movement. It was if someone else was controlling my hand with the streamer in it. I was totally amazed. Something special had just happened. The Holy Spirit took control of my streamer. My question was, "Why now?" I had not asked for His help. I didn't see any danger. Why did He do that? The reason for His intervention this time was not apparent like the other two incidents. I had been praising God. At that moment, I began a seven-year journey to find the reason why the Holy Spirit had taken control of my streamer in church.

A few weeks after the streamer incident, I was led by the Holy Spirit to a worship arts conference called the Joy Conference, where flags were used extensively. On the Friday evening of this conference, the sermon had been preached from the pulpit of a very spacious room. The call was made for the unsaved to come to the altar, and people flocked to the altar. The melodious thumping of tambourines began. A small number of people with flags appeared in the aisles. Then gradually, more people joined them with dancing, more flags, billows, and banners, in the aisles and on the stage. More and more people were coming to the altar. Many chairs were removed to open up the floor space. People were dancing and using flags and banners all over the room. God's presence could definitely be felt in that place.

The following morning, I attended a flag workshop, where I was given some Scriptures about the flags and shown briefly how to handle them. I left the workshop enlightened yet still wanting more understanding and the answer to my question. So I asked God to show me. I asked Him to tell me what He wanted me to know about flags. Five years passed. During one of those five years, I leaned on, trusted, and depended on the Lord for complete healing from cancer. During the other four years, I faced trials from people where my patience and ability to love according to 1 Corinthians 13 were tested. My ability to love was strengthened as I passed tests. You will see how this relates to flags in the chapter on love. I began using flags regularly in church services in 2008.

In 2008, I was moving to music and praising God in church with the flags. I began waving the flags slowly and then slightly faster, while giving God more praise. Both flags did zigzag movements repeatedly up and down in my hands of their own will. The atmosphere all around me seemed to change to a smoky haze. I was staggering like I was drunk. In honor of God's presence, a man lay prostrate on the floor in front of where I was standing. I praised God for making His Holy Spirit's presence known to our congregation that morning. Again, I was amazed.

The Holy Spirit is real. Jesus says, "And I will pray the Father, and He will give you another Helper, that He may abide with you forever, even the Spirit of truth, … but you know Him, for He dwells with you and will be in you" (John 14:16–17 NKJV).

I am a witness that the Holy Spirit is at work with the flags. I am writing this book first to bear witness to the fact that flags are beneficial to the body of Christ, the Church. They are used as a tool by God to bring healing to people by the Holy Spirit's power. Second, I am sharing what I have learned with those who already use the flags. I give careful attention to highlight uses of flags or banners in the Bible and to articulate how those uses are applicable to believers today. I hope to increase or support your understanding on how to use them. I hope this book will be a credit to what flag bearers do in the Church. The words *flag* and *banner* are used interchangeably in this book. Third, I am informing pastors and church leaders that praise and worship with flags are beneficial to the Body of Christ. I encourage church leadership to support their use during worship services. Flags have a biblical purpose to fulfill in the Church. Fourth, I am encouraging others to use the flags at home. This book includes some practical exercises for those who want to get started. Lastly, I want to pique the curiosity and give understanding to those who might never use the flags.

The individual who lifts and waves the flags is waging spiritual warfare. Warfare is when two opposing forces battle against one another with the intent of destroying the opponent. Spiritual warfare is that warfare where the battlefield is in the supernatural realm. One opponent is Satan and his forces. The other opponent is the Lord Jesus and His host of angels. Mankind's supernatural enemy is Satan and his forces. Mankind's help or deliverer to defeat this enemy is the Lord Jesus. Mankind cannot battle this supernatural enemy. Only the supernatural Lord Jesus and His hosts can. Even though this enemy cannot be seen, he is very real and present. Revelations 12:7-9 (KJV) says, "*⁷And there was war in heaven: Michael and his angels fought against the dragon; and the dragon fought and his angels, ⁸And prevailed not; neither was their place found any more in heaven. ⁹And the great dragon was cast out, that old serpent, called the Devil, and Satan, which deceiveth the whole world: he was cast out into the Earth, and his angels were cast out with him.*" Satan is referred to as "*ruler of the kingdom of the air*" in Ephesians 2:2 (NIV). He is referred to as "*prince of this world*" in John 12:30 (NIV).

Satan is our enemy. He "*seeks to steal* (from you), *kill* (you), *and destroy* (your good life)" (John 10:10). The Bible says in 1 Peter 5:8 (KJV), "Be sober, be vigilant; because your adversary the devil, as a roaring lion, walketh about, seeking whom he may devour." He does this by instigating and influencing men to sin. A few of these influences are rebellion, disobedience, insubordination, poverty, violence, sexual immorality, greed, theft, depression, addiction, disease and *"whatever is contrary to the sound doctrine that conforms to the gospel of Jesus Christ."* (The quote is from 1 Timothy 1:10 NIV.) By these means the enemy can and does cause destruction and loss. He wants to destroy relationships within our families, cause us to lose faith in God, cause us to lose hope, finances, health, purpose, peace of mind, and love. He wants to destroy the good life God intended us to have with Him. In the spiritual battle, our goal is to be freed from Satan's influence and defeat the enemy with the Lord Jesus' help. People can call on the Lord Jesus to fight the enemy by asking Him and believing that He will do it.

By the act of calling on the Lord Jesus for His help to defeat this supernatural enemy, we are waging supernatural warfare. One way to call on Him is by getting on our knees and praying. The Holy Spirit led me to another way to wage spiritual warfare. The other way is by giving praise and worship to God combined with prayer and waving the flags to Christian songs.

This form of waging spiritual warfare is ministry or serving a need. An individual may serve the need of him or herself, several people, the family or a congregation of people. The flags may be used in ministry at home or church.

From 2003 until 2010, I learned that there are at least nine factors at work while ministering with the flags. They include the flag bearer, the flag (or any other such instrument like a banner, streamer, or ribbon), prayer, music, color, Scripture (the Truth or God's Word), flag movement and construction, the Holy Spirit, and love.

This text excludes the use of flags for secular purposes such as entertainment, parades, national pride, and the like. This book is the result of prayer, fasting, using the flags, and searching Scriptures. The Holy Spirit led me through the Bible, put people in my path to help me, and most of all gave me amazing experiences with Him and gave others healing while using the flags during worship. I have found that the most pervasive use of the flags is spiritual warfare with prayer to call upon the Master banner—the Lord our God. I got the answers that I was seeking.

This is a living manuscript, in that it will grow as I grow in further understanding and revelation of the flags. I thank the Holy Spirit for showing me the way thus far. I invite you to draw your own conclusions about their use and benefit as you read this book with an understanding heart and a discerning spirit.

Acknowledgments

Thank you, God, for choosing me for this flag ministry and for giving me this work to do in the Earth. Thank you for this assignment to get this teaching into the body of Christ as you gave it to me. Thank you, Holy Spirit, for covering me, leading me, and allowing me to dance under your control while you do your work in the body of Christ. I know you are very real and very present.

Thank you, Helen, for driving and accompanying me to the Joy Conference. You were obedient to God and drove me those five hours. You too were blessed. Thank you, Marcella, for recognizing the anointing on me for flags and giving me the opportunity to develop it within the dance ministry. You freed me to use flags at New Life in Christ (NLC) Interdenominational Church, Lebanon, Illinois, where Bishop Geoffrey V. Dudley, Sr., D. Min is senior pastor. Bishop, thank you for being my covering and letting me do what I have to do with the flags at NLC. Thank you, Lisa, for giving me the freedom to use the flags during worship services.

Pastors Pam and John Dillon, thank you for helping me increase my hearing from God. With that, I am better able to hear and obey the Holy Spirit when He wants to move with the flags. Thank you, Patricia *(sondanceministry.com)*, for all the beautiful silk flags you made and the Scriptures for the colors. Amelda, thank you for your prayers and encouragement. It is you who said I should write this book. Thank you, Bishop Dudley, Teri, Victoria, Jack, Fay and Ann for your review and comments.

1. The Flag Bearer

Flags and banners can be used before a worship service to declare allegiance to God, who is our Banner. We can use the flags to rally and signal the troops (believers in the congregation and forces in the spirit realm) that we are about to engage in spiritual warfare. We are calling on Jesus as the Spirit of the Lord, Jehovah-Tsebaoth, to put our enemy to flight. Sometimes I would stand before the congregation during the invocation with two flags raised, one in each hand. I pray with the flags raised. I call on the Lord of Battles, the Spirit of the Lord.

Flags and banners can be used while you give praise and worship to our Lord, whether at home or in the church. You can use them during praise to bestow great honor to God for the things He has done and for the many victories He has already won. You can use them to worship Him for who He is: Healer, Almighty, King, High Priest, Creator, Redeemer, Conqueror, Refiner, Potter, Life, Peace, the One True God, Love, Alpha and Omega, Provider and more. You can worship all His marvelous traits and characteristics: beautiful, wonderful, glorious, worthy, just, kind, forgiving, gracious, merciful, holy, royal, faithful, righteous, unsleeping, always there, and more. You can use flags while praising God in the dance to exalt the name of the Lord and to give Him all the glory, because thanks be to God, He gives us the victory through our Lord Jesus Christ.

Colossians 2:15 (NIV): "And having disarmed the powers and authorities, he made a public spectacle of them, triumphing over them by the cross."

We use our bodies in giving God praise and as we enter worship. The flag is a tool used as an extension of us. Flags become a part of us as we dance for the Lord. They become an extension of our heart as we focus on Jesus. They enhance our worship. This enhanced worship can be very peaceful and healing for someone watching.

As stated earlier, there are at least nine factors at work in ministering with the flags. The flag bearer is one of those factors. As the term suggests, the flag bearer is the person using the flag. I am one of many flag bearers in this world. In 2009, I was at home dancing with my flags and worshiping God to the song "Worshippers" from the album *Faith Life* by Alvin Slaughter. The Holy Spirit led me in a dance and brought so much peace to me. He compelled me to minister this before people. I danced this same dance at a church in Wildwood, Missouri, in front of people from the Holy Smoke Ministry. The Holy Smoke Ministry is a group of flag bearers who gather monthly to worship God with all their heart, strength, mind, and soul. While I was dancing with the flags, the Holy Spirit covered me completely, all over. It was as if I was in a large, translucent, yet smoky capsule. During the dance, I could see one lady with eyes filled with tears. She wasn't sobbing. Rather, tears were running down her cheeks as she sat and watched.

This is her testimony: "I remember the day you came to Holy Smoke. I was so moved by the presence of God as you moved. The anointing was so strong. Your worship was so peaceful, yet deliberate and purposeful. It appeared to be in slow motion and seemingly choreographed, yet spontaneous, like you knew the song and the dance already. I felt healing flowing, as if through a conduit. I didn't know if it was for you or for us or for someone else someplace else. It was such a worshipful, beautiful thing to watch, and I remember crying as Holy Spirit touched my heart. I remember saying over and over, *Wow* and *beautiful* and *powerful.* I was struck that it was a new revelation for you how powerful in the spirit your flag worship was. I felt that you didn't know at that time how the Lord used your flagging movements in the dance to usher in His glory."

While preparing for a worship service one Wednesday night in 2009, I asked the Holy Spirit to show me what to wear. I was compelled to wear all white garments with a gold cord around my waist and to use a pair of white flags. During that day, Psalm 100:4 NIV—"enter his gates with thanksgiving and his courts with praise"—filled my heart and mouth. I rushed to the church ready to praise the Lord. That night, the Holy Spirit led me to stand in the pulpit instead of on the floor below the pulpit. A worship song was playing over the sanctuary speakers. While in the pulpit, I heard the light hustle, bustle, and chatter of the people as they entered and filled the sanctuary. Oblivious to the congregation, I began moving the flags above me, to the right and left of me, as I turned in a circular pattern. As I moved with the flags, the congregation looked like it was in the background, far away from the pulpit. I seemed to be enclosed in a translucent bubble, holding but not controlling the flag movements. The sounds from the people diminished. The atmosphere changed from busy to quietly calm. Noise and disturbance were lifted from the sanctuary. I saw the praise team form a prayer circle in a small area near the pulpit. They approached, and I moved to the area below the pulpit. Then the praise from the team and the congregation began. I believe the Holy Spirit used the flags. He changed the atmosphere in the sanctuary from busy to calm. He got the people's minds and hearts focused on praise, worship, and the sermon that followed, away from the cares of the day. The Holy Spirit did His work and Psalm 100:4 came alive to me.

It all seems so simple, and it is. However, I have found that there are prerequisites to using the flags effectively in a worship setting. Flags are very attractive and can be very impressive to see in use. However, the goal of using the flag is not just to look good in a worship setting. The main goal of using the flags in praise and worship is to wage spiritual warfare and show people Christ so that He can draw them to Him. In order to accomplish this, there are some preparations you must do before you use the flags in front of a congregation or in your home.

The Flag Bearer

The flag bearer must anoint the flag with oil and dedicate the flag to the Lord—that is, tell God that this flag will only be used to serve Him, and then use it only to serve Him. Set it apart to the Lord to serve His purpose. This is based on Old Testament Scripture for objects set apart for God:

> Exodus 30:25–29 (KJV): [25]And thou shalt make it an oil of holy ointment, an ointment compound after the art of the apothecary: it shall be an holy anointing oil. [26]And thou shalt anoint the tabernacle of the congregation therewith, and the ark of the testimony, [27]And the table and all his vessels, and the candlestick and his vessels, and the altar of incense, [28]And the altar of burnt offering with all his vessels, and the laver and his foot. [29]And thou shalt sanctify them, that they may be most holy: whatsoever toucheth them shall be holy.

The flag bearer must revere and honor God. These flags are instruments to be used *by* Him and *for* Him. When you use them, expect God's presence and help. Expect Him to appear. Ask God to be with you before you use them. Jesus said in John 15:5 (NIV) "apart from me you can do nothing." Be led by the Holy Spirit. Be mindful to go with God, not ahead of Him like the children of Israel did. The people decided to proceed with an attack without God's presence, and the people were defeated. The Israelites went ahead of God, figuratively naked, without His protection and power. In this instance, God was not their banner. God was not the one they followed. Pray to God and always ask the Holy Spirit to lead you.

> Numbers 14:40–45 (NIV): [40] Early the next morning they went up toward the high hill country. "We have sinned," they said. "We will go up to the place the LORD promised." [41] But Moses said, "Why are you disobeying the LORD's command? This will not succeed! [42] Do not go up, because the LORD is not with you. You will be defeated by your enemies, [43] for the Amalekites and Canaanites will face you there. Because you have turned away from the LORD, he will not be with you and you will fall by the sword." [44] Nevertheless, in their presumption they went up toward the high hill country, though neither Moses nor the ark of the LORD's covenant moved from the camp. [45] Then the Amalekites and Canaanites who lived in that hill country came down and attacked them and beat them down all the way to Hormah.

The flag bearer should be baptized with the Holy Spirit. As a born again believer we are baptized by water unto repentance.

> Matthew 3:11 (KJV) says, "I indeed baptize you with water unto repentance. . .

There is another baptism. That baptism is with the Holy Spirit.

> but he that cometh after me is mightier than I, whose shoes I am not worthy to bear: he shall baptize you with the Holy Ghost, and with fire." (Matthew 3:11 (KJV))

With the filling of the Holy Ghost or Spirit also comes power from God so that God's will may be done through us and to us. Here are examples from the Bible where after receiving the Holy Spirit and power, God's will is performed through a person(s):

> "But you will receive power when the Holy Spirit comes on you; and you will be my witnesses in Jerusalem, and in all Judea and Samaria, and to the ends of the earth." (Acts 1:8 NIV)

> "And when they had prayed, the place was shaken where they were assembled together; and they were all filled with the Holy Ghost, and they spake the word of God with boldness." (Acts 4:31 KJV)

> "how God anointed Jesus of Nazareth with the Holy Spirit and power, and how he went around doing good and healing all who were under the power of the devil, because God was with him." (Acts 10:38 NIV)

> ". . . The Holy Spirit will come on you, and the power of the Most High will overshadow you. So the holy one to be born will be called[a] the Son of God." (Luke 1:35 NIV)

A scripture which shows that God's will may be done in us is shown in the following:

> "May the God of hope fill you with all joy and peace as you trust in him, so that you may overflow with hope by the power of the Holy Spirit." (Romans 15:13 NIV)

The flag bearer must be in a position where God's will may be done through the flag bearer. In order to get into that position to be used by God with the flags, the flag bearer should be filled with the Holy Spirit.

It is by the power of the Holy Spirit that God's work is accomplished through us with the flags. One way to receive this baptism of being filled with the Holy Spirit is by praying or asking Jesus to give it to us. We let Jesus know we want to receive the baptism of the Holy Spirit.

Respect yourself. With regard to flags, that means do not compare the way you wave the flag to another person. You may be on a different level of technical ability than the other person. You are all right just where you are. God will grow you. The flag movement is determined a great deal by arm and wrist movements. Each flag bearer's wrist is created differently. So naturally, your flag movement will be different from anyone else's. Be you. God can use you just as you are.

The flag bearer must know who he or she is in Christ, live a life of repentance, love God and other people, and respect him- or herself. Do you know who you are?

The born-again flag bearer is a child of God. He or she is more than a sister, brother, mother, father, teacher, lawyer, accountant, waitress, barber, business owner, volunteer, or any other job title. As children of God, it is important to know who we are in relation to God, because we are engaged in spiritual warfare. As such, we need to know the power we have available to us in order to defeat our enemy. Because you are who you are and you know who you are, you don't bow down to the enemy. You stand up to him. These are a few descriptions of us taken from the New International Version translation of the Bible:

- A wretched man … rescued by Jesus Christ (Rom. 7:24, 25)
- A holy nation (1 Pet. 2:9)
- A royal priesthood (1 Pet. 2:9)
- Member of God's household (Eph. 2:19)
- Fellow citizen with God's people (Eph. 2:19))
- A part of God's whole family in heaven and earth (Eph. 3:15)
- Ambassador for Christ (2 Cor. 5:20)

- You are sent into the world as God sent Jesus into the world (John 17:18)
- Alien and stranger in this world (1 Pet. 2:11)
- The apple of God's eyes (Deut. 32:10)
- You do not belong to the world; Jesus chose you out of the world (John 15:19)
- You live in an earthly tent, and when it is destroyed, you will go to a heavenly house (2 Cor. 5:1)
- A royal diadem in the hand of God (Is. 62:3)

Take the time to meditate and study the above descriptions. Grab hold of their meaning. What do these Scriptures mean to you? How do they change the way you see yourself? Know that you are child of God. As a flag bearer, you must live a life of repentance.

In order to live a life of repentance, you first examine yourself to see your sin (1 John 1:8–10). "If we claim to be without sin, we deceive ourselves and the truth is not in us. If we confess our sins, he is faithful and just and will forgive us our sins and purify us from all unrighteousness. If we claim we have not sinned, we make him out to be a liar and his word has no place in our lives." Examine yourself by comparing yourself against the Bible's description of sin. We are all sinners.

We then purify ourselves by confessing our sins and repenting or turning away from those sins completely. Have a change of heart; make a change toward how God would have you think or act based on His Word. With God's help, this can be done. In doing so, we are acknowledging that God is our focus and everything else revolves around God. We are acknowledging that we depend on Him and not ourselves. This is important for the flag bearer. When the flag bearer's focus is on self, he or she will draw attention to self. When the flag bearer's focus is God, he or she will draw attention to God. Be clean (confess and repent of sin). How can a flag bearer lead a person or a congregation to God if he or she has unrepented sin? Who can ascend the holy hill to get into God's presence? He who has clean hands and a pure heart. Psalm 24:1–4 NIV says:

> [1] The earth is the LORD's, and everything in it, the world, and all who live in it; [2] for he founded it upon the seas and established it upon the waters. [3] Who may ascend the hill of the LORD? Who may stand in his holy place? [4] He who has clean hands and a pure heart, who does not lift up his soul to an idol or swear by what is false.

Only touch the flags with clean hands and a pure heart. How do you become clean? You become clean by washing as Moses did whenever he entered the Tent of Meeting.

> Exodus 40:30–35 (NIV): [30] [Moses] placed the basin between the Tent of Meeting and the altar and put water in it for washing, [31] and Moses and Aaron and his sons used it to wash their hands and feet. [32] They washed whenever they entered the Tent of Meeting or approached the altar, as the LORD commanded Moses. [33] Then Moses set up the courtyard around the tabernacle and altar and put up the curtain at the entrance to the courtyard. And so Moses finished the work. [34] Then the cloud covered the Tent of Meeting, and the glory of the LORD filled the tabernacle. [35] Moses could not enter the Tent of Meeting because the cloud had settled upon it, and the glory of the LORD filled the tabernacle.

God's presence was at the Tent of Meeting. The basin was made of mirrors. As they used the basin, they could see their reflection in the mirrors. They washed themselves with water from that basin every time they entered the tent, the place of God's presence. Today we wash ourselves by the Word before going to a place where God abides. To be washed by the Word means to sanctify ourselves with the Word. John 17:17 (NIV) says, "Sanctify them by the truth; your word is truth." We do not think like nor behave like people in the world who do not know the Word. The Bible or the Word is the absolute Truth. It speaks what is real. We accept It as It is. There can be no compromises to what the Bible says nor means. To be washed by the Word means to examine, assess, compare, and see ourselves against the teachings of the Bible (the Word). We then apply the Word to our lifestyles and to the choices we make in every area of our lives. With the help of the Holy Spirit, keep our hearts free from envy, strife, pride, jealousy, offense, disobedience, lust, sodomy, witchcraft, unforgiveness, addiction, control, manipulation, contention, division, greed, rage, idolatry, selfishness, criticism, hate, murder, revenge, sexual immorality and the like. Furthermore, obey God's commands.

The greatest commands are to love God and love others. They are the two most important commandments in the Bible. Mark 12: 30–31 NIV says:

> [30] "Love the Lord your God with all your heart and with all your soul and with all your mind and with all your strength." [31] The second is this: "Love your neighbor as yourself." There is no commandment greater than these.

When we are washed by the Word, then we are most definitely washed by these two commandments. Love is the major cleansing ingredient. You are seeking to get into the presence of God. That is why it is so important to know what love is.

2. Love

The Bible tells us to love, many times and in many ways. Love. Love. Love. This is most important, whether we wave the flag or not. It is particularly important to flag bearers. Without our love toward others, we are nothing. A person can wave the flags, but without love, that's all he or she is doing. Without love, we will not be able to touch or reach the heart of the person(s) we are ministering to (the person(s) watching you). Nor will we be able to enter the presence of God. It is likened to 1 Corinthians 13:1 (NIV), which says "If I speak in the tongues of men and of angels, but have not love, I am only a resounding gong or a clanging cymbal."

The most important concept flag bearers (those who carry the banners) must understand is love, because God is the master Banner and His banner is love:

God is love.

Jesus says "come, follow me" (Matt. 4:19 NIV).

The Lord is *our* banner.

Follow that Banner.

Keep your eye on that Banner.

When we follow that Banner which is over us, we follow God.

When we follow God, we follow love.

When we follow love, we walk in the way of love.
God tells us to walk this way for our own protection.
When love is present, evil and hate have to disappear.

Aside from loving God, the most important lesson a flag bearer must learn is how to show love to others. If we wave flags to music with the most beautiful choreography and execute the finest techniques but have not love, we are nothing and gain nothing. We have not ministered to anyone. First Corinthians 13:2, 3, 8, 10 says:

[2] If I have the gift of prophecy and can fathom all mysteries and all knowledge, and if I have a faith that can move mountains, but have not love, I am nothing. [3] If I give all I possess to the poor and surrender my body to the flames, but have not love, I gain nothing. … [8] Love never fails. … [10] but when perfection comes, the imperfect disappears.

Know what love is according to 1 Corinthians 13. The New American Standard Bible version is an excellent interpretation of this chapter. Walk in this teaching. How are your ways compared to love's ways? Do you know what love is when you see it? Do not take it lightly that you know what love is just because you have heard or used that word many times, or that you think you know what it is because you have experienced feelings of "love." This kind of love God speaks of is not an emotion. Love is a commitment to treat people the way God tells us to treat them. You will know what real love is when you have walked it and followed it according to the Bible. We must practice it every day; in other words, put it into action, no matter what. Never become tired of it. Grow in it. When we slip and fall down in this walk, we get up and get going in it again. Forget what is behind, and strain toward what is ahead; "press on toward the goal to win the prize for which God has called" (Phil. 3:14 NIV) you heavenward in Christ Jesus. With the help of God the Father, the Son, and the Holy Spirit, we'll attain it.

Evangelist Henry Drummond (1851 –1897) wrote an essay entitled "The Greatest Thing in the World." He gives an eloquent explanation of how love presents itself in action, how you should treat others, and how you should behave, based on 1 Corinthians 13.

As you read Evangelist Drummond's excerpt below, underline the behaviors. Which ones describe you? Which ones do you need to put into practice? Will you practice the behaviors that show love? With the help of Jesus Christ, will you choose to grow up in love? This passage helped me to recognize that I was not showing love according to 1 Corinthians 13. The article helped me to see that I still had some growing to do in love. God tested me severely and let trials come my way during the five-year period from 2003 to 2008. I have grown, and I am still practicing it. Practice what Evangelist Drummond preached over a hundred years ago, and see the difference it makes in you.

Love by Henry Drummond

> The Spectrum of Love has nine ingredients:
> Patience . . . . . . "Love suffereth long."
> Kindness . . . . . . "And is kind."
> Generosity . . . . "Love envieth not."
> Humility . . . . . . "Love vaunteth not itself, is not puffed up."
> Courtesy . . . . . . "Doth not behave itself unseemly."
> Unselfishness . . "Seeketh not her own."
> Good Temper . . "Is not easily provoked."
> Guilelessness . . "Thinketh no evil."
> Sincerity . . . . . . "Rejoiceth not in iniquity, but rejoiceth in the truth."
>
> There is no time to do more than make a passing note upon each of these ingredients. 1. Love is Patience. This is the normal attitude of Love; Love passive, Love waiting to begin; not in a hurry; calm; ready to do its work when the summons comes, but meantime wearing

the ornament of a meek and quiet spirit. Love suffers long; beareth all things; believeth all things; hopeth all things. For Love understands, and therefore waits.

2. Kindness. Love active. Have you ever noticed how much of Christ's life was spent in doing kind things—in merely doing kind things? Run over it with that in view and you will find that He spent a great proportion of His time simply in making people happy, in doing good turns to people. There is only one thing greater than happiness in the world, and that is holiness; and it is not in our keeping; but what God has put in our power is the happiness of those about us, and that is largely to be secured by our being kind to them.

"The greatest thing," says someone, "a man can do for his Heavenly Father is to be kind to some of His other children." I wonder why it is that we are not all kinder than we are? How much the world needs it. How easily it is done. How instantaneously it acts. How infallibly it is remembered. How superabundantly it pays itself back--for there is no debtor in the world so honourable, so superbly honourable, as Love. "Love never faileth". Love is success, Love is happiness, Love is life.

Where Love is, God is. He that dwelleth in Love dwelleth in God. God is love. Therefore love. Without distinction, without calculation, without procrastination, love. Lavish it upon the poor, where it is very easy; especially upon the rich, who often need it most; most of all upon our equals, where it is very difficult, and for whom perhaps we each do least of all. There is a difference between trying to please and giving pleasure. Give pleasure. Lose no chance of giving pleasure. For that is the ceaseless and anonymous triumph of a truly loving spirit.

3. Generosity. "Love envieth not." This is Love in competition with others. Whenever you attempt a good work you will find other men doing the same kind of work, and probably doing it better. Envy them not. Envy is a feeling of ill-will to those who are in the same line as ourselves, a spirit of covetousness and detraction. How little Christian work even is a protection against un-Christian feeling. That most despicable of all the unworthy moods which cloud a Christian's soul assuredly waits for us on the threshold of every work, unless we are fortified with this grace of magnanimity. Only one thing truly need the Christian envy, the large, rich, generous soul which "envieth not."

4. And then, after having learned all that, you have to learn this further thing, Humility—to put a seal upon your lips and forget what you have done. After you have been kind, after Love has stolen forth into the world and done its beautiful work, go back into the shade again and say nothing about it Love hides even from itself. Love waives even self-satisfaction. "Love vaunteth not itself, is not puffed up."

5. The fifth ingredient is a somewhat strange one to find in this *summum bonum:* Courtesy. This is Love in society, Love in relation to etiquette. "Love doth not behave itself unseemly." Politeness has been defined as

15

love in trifles. Courtesy is said to be love in little things. And the one secret of politeness is to love. Love cannot behave itself unseemly. You can put the most untutored person into the highest society, and if they have a reservoir of love in their heart, they will not behave themselves unseemly. They simply cannot do it. Carlyle said of Robert Burns that there was no truer gentleman in Europe than the ploughman-poet. It was because he loved everything—the mouse, and the daisy, and all the things, great and small, that God had made. So with this simple passport he could mingle with any society, and enter courts and palaces from his little cottage on the banks of the Ayr. You know the meaning of the word "gentleman." It means a gentle man—a man who does things gently, with love. And that is the whole art and mystery of it. The gentleman cannot in the nature of things do an ungentle, an ungentlemanly thing. The un-gentle soul, the inconsiderate, unsympathetic nature cannot do anything else. "Love doth not behave itself unseemly."

6. Unselfishness. "Love seeketh not her own." Observe: Seeketh not even that which is her own. In Britain the Englishman is devoted, and rightly, to his rights. But there come times when a man may exercise even the higher right of giving up his rights. Yet Paul does not summon us to give up our rights. Love strikes much deeper. It would have us not seek them at all, ignore them, eliminate the personal element altogether from our calculations. It is not hard to give up our rights. They are often external. The difficult thing is to give up ourselves. The more difficult thing still is not to seek

things for ourselves at all. After we have sought them, bought them, won them, deserved them, we have taken the cream off them for ourselves already. Little cross then, perhaps, to give them up. But not to seek them, to look every man not on his own things, but on the things of others--id opus est. "Seekest thou great things for thyself?" said the prophet; "seek them not." Why? Because there is no greatness in things. Things cannot be great. The only greatness is unselfish love. Even self-denial in itself is nothing, is almost a mistake. Only a great purpose or a mightier love can justify the waste. It is more difficult, I have said, not to seek our own at all, than, having sought it, to give it up. I must take that back. It is only true of a partly selfish heart. Nothing is a hardship to Love, and nothing is hard. I believe that Christ's yoke is easy. Christ's "yoke" is just His way of taking life. And I believe it is an easier way than any other. I believe it is a happier way than any other. The most obvious lesson in Christ's teaching is that there is no happiness in having and getting anything, but only in giving. I repeat, there is no happiness in having or in getting, but only in giving. And half the world is on the wrong scent in the pursuit of happiness. They think it consists in having and getting, and in being served by others. It consists in giving, and in serving others. He that would be great among you, said Christ, let him serve. He that would be happy, let him remember that there is but one way—it is more blessed, it is more happy, to give than to receive.

7. The next ingredient is a very remarkable one: Good Temper. "Love is not easily provoked." Nothing could be

more striking than to find this here. We are inclined to look upon bad temper as a very harmless weakness. We speak of it as a mere infirmity of nature, a family failing, a matter of temperament, not a thing to take into very serious account in estimating a man's character. And yet here, right in the heart of this analysis of love, it finds a place; and the Bible again and again returns to condemn it as one of the most destructive elements in human nature.

The peculiarity of ill temper is that it is the vice of the virtuous. It is often the one blot on an otherwise noble character. You know men who are all but perfect, and women who would be entirely perfect, but for an easily ruffled, quick-tempered, or "touchy" disposition. This compatibility of ill temper with high moral character is one of the strangest and saddest problems of ethics. The truth is there are two great classes of sins—sins of the Body, and sins of the Disposition. The Prodigal Son may be taken as a type of the first, the Elder Brother of the second. Now society has no doubt whatever as to which of these is the worse. Its brand falls, without a challenge, upon the Prodigal. But are we right? We have no balance to weigh one another's sins, and coarser and finer are but human words; but faults in the higher nature may be less venial than those in the lower, and to the eye of Him who is Love, a sin against Love may seem a hundred times more base. No form of vice, not worldliness, not greed of gold, not drunkenness itself, does more to un-Christianise society than evil temper. For embittering life, for breaking up communities, for destroying the most sacred relationships, for devastating homes, for withering up men and women, for taking the bloom off childhood; in short, for sheer gratuitous misery-producing power, this influence stands alone. Look at the Elder Brother, moral, hard-working, patient, dutiful—let him get all credit for his virtues--look at this man, this baby, sulking outside his own father's door. "He was angry," we read, "and would not go in." Look at the effect upon the father, upon the servants, upon the happiness of the guests. Judge of the effect upon the Prodigal—and how many prodigals are kept out of the Kingdom of God by the unlovely characters of those who profess to be inside? Analyze, as a study in Temper, the thunder-cloud itself as it gathers upon the Elder Brother's brow. What is it made of? Jealousy, anger, pride, uncharity, cruelty, self-righteousness, touchiness, doggedness, sullenness—these are the ingredients of this dark and loveless soul. In varying proportions, also, these are the ingredients of all ill temper. Judge if such sins of the disposition are not worse to live in, and for others to live with, than sins of the body. Did Christ indeed not answer the question Himself when He said, "I say unto you, that the publicans and the harlots go into the Kingdom of Heaven before you." There is really no place in Heaven for a disposition like this. A man with such a mood could only make Heaven miserable for all the people in it. Except, therefore, such a man be born again, he cannot, he simply cannot, enter the Kingdom of Heaven. For it is perfectly certain—and you will not misunderstand me--that to enter Heaven a man must take it with him.

You will see then why Temper is significant. It is not in what it is alone, but in what it reveals. This is why I take the liberty now of speaking of it with such unusual plainness. It is a test for love, a symptom, a revelation of an unloving nature at bottom. It is the intermittent fever which bespeaks unintermittent disease within; the occasional bubble escaping to the surface which betrays some rottenness underneath; a sample of the most hidden products of the soul dropped involuntarily when off one's guard; in a word, the lightning form of a hundred hideous and un-Christian sins. For a want of patience, a want of kindness, a want of generosity, a want of courtesy, a want of unselfishness, are all instantaneously symbolised in one flash of Temper.

Hence it is not enough to deal with the temper. We must go to the source, and change the inmost nature, and the angry humours will die away of themselves. Souls are made sweet not by taking the acid fluids out, but by putting something in—a great Love, a new Spirit, the Spirit of Christ. Christ, the Spirit of Christ, interpenetrating ours, sweetens, purifies, transforms all. This only can eradicate what is wrong, work a chemical change, renovate and regenerate, and rehabilitate the inner man. Will-power does not change men. Time does not change men. Christ does. Therefore "Let that mind be in you which was also in Christ Jesus." Some of us have not much time to lose. Remember, once more, that this is a matter of life or death. I cannot help speaking urgently, for myself, for yourselves. "Whoso shall offend one of these little ones, which believe in me, it were better for him that a millstone were hanged about his neck, and that he were drowned in the depth of the sea." That is to say, it is the deliberate verdict of the Lord Jesus that it is better not to live than not to love. It is better not to live than not to love.

8. Guilelessness and Sincerity may be dismissed almost with a word. Guilelessness is the grace for suspicious people. And the possession of it is the great secret of personal influence. You will find, if you think for a moment, that the people who influence you are people who believe in you. In an atmosphere of suspicion men shrivel up; but in that atmosphere they expand, and find encouragement and educative fellowship. It is a wonderful thing that here and there in this hard, uncharitable world there should still be left a few rare souls who think no evil. This is the great unworldliness. Love "thinketh no evil," imputes no motive, sees the bright side, puts the best construction on every action. What a delightful state of mind to live in! What a stimulus and benediction even to meet with it for a day! To be trusted is to be saved. And if we try to influence or elevate others, we shall soon see that success is in proportion to their belief of our belief in them. For the respect of another is the first restoration of the self-respect a man has lost; our ideal of what he is becomes to him the hope and pattern of what he may become.

9. "Love rejoiceth not in iniquity, but rejoiceth in the truth." I have called this Sincerity from the words rendered in the Authorised Version by "rejoiceth in the truth." And, certainly, were this the real translation, nothing could be more just. For he who loves will love

Truth not less than men. He will rejoice in the Truth—
rejoice not in what he has been taught to believe; not in
this Church's doctrine or in that; not in this ism or in
that ism; but "in the Truth." He will accept only what
is real; he will strive to get at facts; he will search for
Truth with a humble and unbiased mind, and cherish
whatever he finds at any sacrifice. But the more literal
translation of the Revised Version calls for just such a
sacrifice for truth's sake here. For what Paul really meant
is, as we there read, "Rejoiceth not in unrighteousness,
but rejoiceth with the truth," a quality which probably
no one English word—and certainly not Sincerity—
adequately defines. It includes, perhaps more strictly,
the self-restraint which refuses to make capital out of
others' faults; the charity which delights not in exposing
the weakness of others, but "covereth all things"; the
sincerity of purpose which endeavours to see things as
they are, and rejoices to find them better than suspicion
feared or calumny denounced.

So much for the analysis of Love. Now the business of
our lives is to have these things fitted into our characters.
That is the supreme work to which we need to address
ourselves in this world, to learn Love. Is life not full of
opportunities for learning Love? Every man and woman
every day has a thousand of them. The world is not a
play-ground; it is a schoolroom. Life is not a holiday,
but an education. And the one eternal lesson for us all
is how better we can love. What makes a man a good
cricketer? Practice. What makes a man a good artist, a
good sculptor, a good musician? Practice. What makes
a man a good linguist, a good stenographer? Practice.

What makes a man a good man? Practice. Nothing else. There is nothing capricious about religion. We do not get the soul in different ways, under different laws, from those in which we get the body and the mind. If a man does not exercise his arm he develops no biceps muscle; and if a man does not exercise his soul, he acquires no muscle in his soul, no strength of character, no vigour of moral fibre, nor beauty of spiritual growth. Love is not a thing of enthusiastic emotion. It is a rich, strong, manly, vigorous expression of the whole round Christian character—the Christlike nature in its fullest development. And the constituents of this great character are only to be built up by ceaseless practice."

Now that you have read and examined yourself, know this: There is a connection between God and our using flags. That connection is love. You must have clean hands and a pure heart to get into God's presence. You become clean by confessing your sin and repenting. After you repent, walk in love. It's when you are in His presence that He can do His work with the flag.

When you are using the flags, loving God and people is the most important prerequisite to using the flag. It's a matter of the heart. If you want people to see Christ, He must be in your heart. He is love. Love must be in your heart.

3. Biblical Uses of Flags

The flag of today is an equivalent for the banner and standard used during biblical times. The uses of these banners and standards are rooted in the Bible. Their first uses for God's people can be found in the Old Testament. They were used to indicate to whom they belonged, to mark a rallying point, to send a signal, to herald an event, and to bestow honor to God.

Represent to Whom You Belong

The first use of flags in the Bible can be found in Numbers 2:1–34 (NIV). God told the people to camp under their standard. When the Israelites set out from camp, each tribe and division of Israel assembled around its unique standard with the banners. Their identity and to what tribe they belonged was recognized by their standard.

[1] The LORD said to Moses and Aaron: [2] "The Israelites are to camp around the Tent of Meeting some distance from it, each man under his standard with the banners (KJV ensign) of his family (KJV father's house)." [3] On the east, toward the sunrise, the divisions of the camp of Judah are to encamp under their standard ... [10] On the south will be the divisions of the camp of Reuben under their standard.... They will set out second. [17] Then the Tent of Meeting and the camp of the Levites will set out in the middle of the camps. They will set out in the same order as

they encamp, each in his own place under his standard. [18] On the west will be the divisions of the camp of Ephraim under their standard. ... [25] On the north will be the divisions of the camp of Dan, under their standard. .... [34] So the Israelites did everything the LORD commanded Moses; that is the way they encamped under their standards, and that is the way they set out, each with his clan and family.

The Meaning of Standard and Banner

The Holy Bible New International Version uses two terms, *standard* and *banner,* which are closely related. The *Unger's Bible Dictionary*[1] defines a *standard* as a figure or device of some kind elevated on a pole. God's people were not the only people to use standards during Old Testament times. The Egyptians had theirs. Pictures of Israel's standards are not available. Pictured below are Egyptian standards of that era:

The *Unger's Bible Dictionary* defines a *banner* as "something conspicuous or easily seen; *standards* or symbols erected on poles, hilltops or other conspicuous places to rally tribes or armies." Psalm 20:5 KJV uses the phrase "set up our banners." The *Hebrew and*

---

1   *Unger's Bible Dictionary,* Moody Press, copyright 1985, ISBN 0–8024–9035–2.

Chaldee Dictionary[2] (1713) defines this phrase as "dagal, to flaunt, i.e., raise a flag."

The King James Version of the Bible uses the term *ensign* in place of *banner* in Numbers 2:2:

> *"Every man of the children of Israel shall pitch by his own standard, with the ensign of their father's house: far off about the tabernacle of the congregation shall they pitch."*

The *Lexical Aid to the Old Testament*[3] (226) says an ensign is an "oth," which is *"a sign, symbol, standard, miracle, banner."* Oth grabbed my attention and curiosity. One of the most interesting facts I found is that oth appears in one of the names of God, Lord of Sabaoth. Lord of Sabaoth is used in Romans 9:29 KJV.

Romans 9:29 KJV says, "And as Esaias said before, Except the Lord of Sabaoth had left us a seed, we had been as Sodoma, and been made like unto Gomorrha."

I became fascinated in the name of God as Lord of Sabaoth in my search to find out why the Holy Spirit had taken control of my streamer (a flag-like tool). So I delved into Lord of Sabaoth. I found that *Lord* means *supreme in authority. Greek Dictionary of the New Testament*[4] says *"Sabaoth (4519) is of Hebrew origin meaning 'armies'; i.e. tsebaoth, a military epithet of God."* The *Unger's Bible Dictionary* defines Sabaoth as *"supreme head and commander of all the heavenly forces; the angels who are the Lord's agents are ever ready to execute the Lord's will."* Our Lord

---

2   *Hebrew Greek Key Study Bible,* King James Version, *Hebrew and Chaldee Dictionary,* Zodhiates, World Bible Publishers, Inc. Revised Edition, Second Printing, October 1992, copyright 1984 and 1991.

3   *Hebrew Greek Key Study Bible,* King James Version, *Lexical Aid to the Old Testament,* Zodhiates, World Bible Publishers, Inc. Revised Edition, Second Printing, October 1992, copyright 1984 and 1991.

4   *Hebrew Greek Key Study Bible,* King James Version, *Greek Dictionary of the New Testament,* Zodhiates, World Bible Publishers, Inc. Revised Edition, Second Printing, October 1992, copyright 1984 and 1991.

is the Lord of Armies (heavenly armies), God of Hosts. Our Lord is Jehovah Tsebaoth.

Tsebaoth is the combination of the primary root word "tsaba" + "oth." The *Hebrew and Chaldee Dictionary* 6634 says *"tseba corresponds to tsaba in the figurative sense of summoning one's wishes; will."* The *Hebrew and Chaldee Dictionary* 6633 says *"the Hebrew word 'tsaba' is a primary root; to mass (an army or servants):—assemble, fight, perform, muster, war."* Oth is a banner. A banner is a flag. Oth is raising God in a figurative way to go before us in battle. Oth is a big part of who God is. Oth is such a big part that it is a part of one of His glorious names, Lord of Sabaoth or Jehovah Tsebaoth the Lord of Armies or Lord of Hosts.

To Mark a Rallying Point

Isaiah 11:10–16 (The Message) says the people will rally together! The banner will show them where to come together. The banner marked the rallying point.

[10] On that day, Jesse's Root will be raised high, posted as a rallying banner for the peoples. The nations will all come to him. His headquarters will be glorious. [11] Also on that day, the Master for the second time will reach out to bring back what's left of his scattered people. He'll bring them back from Assyria, Egypt, Pathros, Ethiopia, Elam, Sinar, Hamath, and the ocean islands. [12-16] And he'll raise that rallying banner high, visible to all nations, gather in all the scattered exiles of Israel, Pull in all the dispersed refugees of Judah from the four winds and the seven seas.… In the end there'll be a highway all the way from Assyria, easy traveling for what's left of God's people—A highway just like the one Israel had when he marched up out of Egypt.

To Send a Signal

Isaiah 5:25–30 (The Message) shows how the flag was used to send a signal.

²⁵⁻³⁰ That's why God flamed out in anger against his people, reached out and knocked them down.

The mountains trembled as their dead bodies piled up in the streets. But even after that, he was still angry, his fist still raised, ready to hit them again. He raises a flag, <u>signaling a distant nation</u>, whistles for people at the ends of the earth. And here they come—on the run! None drag their feet, no one stumbles, no one sleeps or dawdles. Shirts are on and pants buckled, every boot is spit-polished and tied. Their arrows are sharp, bows strung, The hooves of their horses shod, chariot wheels greased.... Every light in the sky will be blacked out by the clouds.

To Herald an Event

Isaiah 18:1–7 (The Message) shows how the flag was used to herald an event.

¹⁻² Doom to the land of flies and mosquitoes beyond the Ethiopian rivers, Shipping emissaries all over the world, down rivers and across seas. Go, swift messengers, go to this people tall and handsome, This people held in respect everywhere, this people mighty and merciless, from the land crisscrossed with rivers. 3 Everybody everywhere, all earth-dwellers: <u>When you see a flag flying on the mountain, look! When you hear the trumpet blown, listen!</u> ⁴⁻⁶ For here's what God told me: "I'm not going to say anything, but simply look on from where I live, Quiet as warmth that comes from the sun, silent as dew during harvest." ... ⁷ Then tribute will be brought to God-of-the-Angel-Armies, brought from this people tall and handsome, This people once

29

held in respect everywhere, this people once mighty and merciless, From the land crisscrossed with rivers, to Mount Zion, God's place.

To Bestow Honor to God

Another use of banners was to bestow great honor to God. Moses dedicated an altar to the Lord and named it Jehovah-Nissi (the Lord is my Banner (Exodus 17:15 NIV)) "because the Lord hath sworn that the Lord will have war with Amalek from generation to generation" (KJV). According to the *Unger's Bible Dictionary,* it has been suggested that the altar with its expressive name was merely to serve as a memorial to posterity of the gracious help of Jehovah.

Exodus 17:9–16 (KJV): [9]And Moses said unto Joshua, Choose us out men, and go out, fight with Amalek: tomorrow I will stand on the top of the hill with the rod of God in mine hand. [10] So Joshua did as Moses had said to him, and fought with Amalek: and Moses, Aaron, and Hur went up to the top of the hill. [11] And it came to pass, when Moses held up his hand, that Israel prevailed: and when he let down his hand, Amalek prevailed. [12] But Moses' hands were heavy; and they took a stone, and put it under him, and he sat thereon; and Aaron and Hur stayed up his hands, the one on the one side, and the other on the other side; and his hands were steady until the going down of the sun. [13] And Joshua discomfited Amalek and his people with the edge of the sword. [14] And the LORD said unto Moses, Write this for a memorial in a book, and rehearse it in the ears of Joshua: for I will utterly put out the remembrance of Amalek from under heaven. [15] And Moses built an altar, and called the name of it Jehovah-Nissi: [16] For he said, Because the LORD hath sworn that the LORD will have war with Amalek from generation to generation.

Also pertinent to today's use of flags is color, which can be seen quite often in the Old Testament.

4. Color

The Scriptures are full of references to color. As you scratch below the surface of verses, you can see what certain colors could represent. Colors are symbols. So how is color a factor while ministering with the flags? In an earlier chapter, I talked about a banner being a standard or symbol erected on a pole. The color is the symbol or standard raised on a pole. Flag colors are symbolic of the nature, name, or attribute of the Lord. When we raise and wave a flag of a particular color, we are raising a symbol of a particular attribute of God or one of His names. Also, while raising this standard, we are claiming to belong to who or what the symbol represents. All those who belonged to or who were a part of the house of Judah encamped under the symbol or standard of Judah (Numbers 2:3). Here is an example of how this may be used in ministry. Ezekiel 47:12 says "leaves will serve for healing."

> Ezekiel 47:12 (NIV): Fruit trees of all kinds will grow on both banks of the river. Their leaves will not wither, nor will their fruit fail. Every month they will bear, because the water from the sanctuary flows to them. Their fruit will serve for food and their leaves for healing.

Leaves are green. Green could be associated with healing. God is Healer. When we raise a green flag, we are raising a standard or symbol that shows God's attribute of Healer. We are also showing that we belong to God who is Healer.

As another example, purple could be associated with authority in Daniel 5:29 and royalty or kingship in Esther 8:15:

> Authority: Daniel 5:29 (NASB): Then Belshazzar gave orders, and they clothed Daniel with <u>purple</u> and put a necklace of gold around his neck, and issued a proclamation concerning him that he now had <u>authority</u> as the third ruler in the kingdom.

> Royalty, kingship: Esther 8:15 (NIV): Mordecai left the <u>king's</u> presence wearing <u>royal</u> garments of blue and white, a large crown of gold and a purple robe of fine linen. And the city of Susa held a joyous celebration.

When we raise a purple flag, we are raising a standard or symbol that shows God has authority and royalty and is King. When I raise a purple flag, I am declaring God is my King and that He has all authority over everything. I am identifying with the God who is all-majestic. We can ask God to tell us or show us what color flags to use. The following pages show some colors that could be used.

Purple

Beauty: Ez. 27:3,7 (KJV): "[3] O Tyrus, thou hast said, I am of perfect beauty . . . [7] Fine linen with broidered work from Egypt was that which thou spreadest forth to be thy sail; blue and purple from the isles of Elishah was that which covered thee."

Red

Life: Lev. 17:11 (NIV): "For the life of a creature is in the blood, and I have given it to you to make atonement for yourselves on the altar; it is the blood that makes atonement for one's life."

Judgment or Redemption: Isa. 63:2–4 (NIV): "² why are your garments red, like those of one treading the winepress? ³ I have trodden the winepress alone; from the nations no one was with me. I trampled them in my anger and trod them down in my wrath; their blood spattered my garments, and I stained all my clothing. ⁴ For the day of vengeance was in my heart, and the year of my redemption has come."

Forgiveness: Matt. 26:28 (NIV): "This is my blood of the covenant, which is poured out for many for the forgiveness of sins."

War: Nahum 2:3 (NIV): "The shields of his soldiers are red; the warriors are clad in scarlet."

Power: Rev. 6:4 (NIV): "Then another horse came out, a fiery red one. Its rider was given power to take peace from the earth and to make men slay each other. To him was given a large sword."

Leaf Green

Healing: Rev. 22:1–2 (NIV): "¹ Then the angel showed me the river of the water of life, as clear as crystal, flowing from the throne of God and of the Lamb ² down the middle of the great street of the city. On each side of the river stood the tree of life, bearing twelve crops of fruit, yielding its fruit every month. And the leaves of the tree are for the healing of the nations."

Life: John 15:5 (NIV): "I am the vine; you are the branches. If a man remains in me and I in him, he will bear much fruit; apart from me you can do nothing."

Fruitful, the Fruit of the Spirit: Ps. 92:12–13 (NIV): "¹² The righteous will flourish like a palm tree, they will grow like a cedar of Lebanon; ¹³ planted in the house of the LORD, they will flourish in the courts of our God."

Fruitful, the Fruit of the Spirit: Hosea 14:8 (NIV) "I am like a green pine tree; your fruitfulness comes from me."

Light Green

New Life; New Beginnings: Job 8:11–12 (KJV): "[11] Can the rush grow up without mire? Can the flag grow without water? [12] Whilst it is yet in his greenness, and not cut down, it withereth before any other herb."

Emerald Rainbow

Throne of God: Rev. 4:3 (NIV): "And the one who sat there had the appearance of jasper and carnelian. A rainbow, resembling an emerald, encircled the throne."

Rainbow

Radiance, Glory: Ezek. 1:28 (NIV): "Like the appearance of a rainbow in the clouds on a rainy day, so was the radiance around him. This was the appearance of the likeness of the glory of the LORD. When I saw it, I fell facedown, and I heard the voice of one speaking."

Olive Green

Anointing: Ex. 30:24, 25, 29 (KJV): "[24] … and of olive an hin: [25] And thou shalt make it an oil of holy ointment … it shall be an holy anointing oil.… [29] And thou shalt sanctify them, that they may be most holy: whatsoever toucheth them shall be holy."

Breakthrough: Is. 10:27 (KJV): "And it shall come to pass in that day, that his burden shall be taken away from off thy shoulder, and his yoke from off thy neck, and the yoke shall be destroyed because of the anointing."

Healing: Mark 6:13 (NIV): "They drove out many demons and anointed many sick people with oil and healed them."

Holy Spirit: 1 John 2:20, 27 (NIV): "But you have an anointing from the Holy One, and all of you know the truth.… As for you, the anointing you received from him remains in you, and you do not need anyone to teach you. But as his anointing teaches you about all things and as that anointing is real, not counterfeit—just as it has taught you, remain in him."

Bright Yellow

Light: John 8:12 (NIV): "When Jesus spoke again to the people, he said, 'I am the light of the world. Whoever follows me will never walk in darkness, but will have the light of life.'"

Joy: Ps. 21:6 (NIV): "Surely you have granted him eternal blessings and made him glad with the joy of your presence."

White

Holy, Undefiled, Worthy, Victorious: Rev. 3:4–5 (KJV): "⁴ Thou hast a few names even in Sardis which have not defiled their garments; and they shall walk with me in white: for they are worthy. ⁵ He that overcometh, the same shall be clothed in white raiment."

Sacred: Daniel 7:9 (NIV): "As I looked, thrones were set in place, and the Ancient of Days took his seat. His clothing was as white as snow; the hair of his head was white like wool."

Honor and Righteousness: Rev. 19:7–8 (KJV): "⁷ Let us be glad and rejoice, and give honor to him: for the marriage of the Lamb is come, and his wife hath made herself ready. ⁸ And to her was granted that she should be arrayed in fine linen, clean and white: for the fine linen is the righteousness of saints."

Glory: Rev. 21:10–11 (NIV): "[10] And he carried me away in the Spirit to a mountain great and high, and showed me the Holy City, Jerusalem, coming down out of heaven from God. [11]It shone with the glory of God, and its brilliance was like that of a very precious jewel, like a jasper, clear as crystal."

Gold

Kingship: Esther 8:4 (NIV): "Then the king extended the gold scepter to Esther and she arose and stood before him."

Refiner: Mal. 3:3 (NIV): "He will sit as a refiner and purifier of silver; he will purify the Levites and refine them like gold and silver."

Wisdom: Prov. 25:12 (NASB) "Like an earring of gold and an ornament of fine gold is a wise reprover to a listening ear."

Iron

Weapon for Battle: Ps. 2:8–9 (KJV): "[8] Ask of me, and I shall give thee the heathen for thine inheritance ... [9] Thou shalt break them with a rod of iron; thou shalt dash them in pieces like a potter's vessel."

The Word: Rev. 19:15 (KJV): "And out of his mouth goeth a sharp sword, that with it he should smite the nations: and he shall rule them with a rod of iron: and he treadeth the winepress of the fierceness and wrath of Almighty God."

Power and Strength: Rev. 2:26–27 (KJV): "[26] And he that overcometh, and keepeth my works unto the end, to him will I give power over the nations: [27] And he shall rule them with a rod of iron; as the vessels of a potter shall they be broken to shivers: even as I received of my Father."

Silver

Word: Ps. 12:6 (NIV): "And the words of the LORD are flawless, like silver refined in a furnace of clay, purified seven times."

God's Refining Process: Ps. 66:10 (KJV): "For thou, O God, hast proved us: thou hast tried us, as silver is tried." Redemption: Luke 15:8–10 (KJV): "⁸ Either what woman having ten pieces of silver, if she lose one piece, doth not light a candle, and sweep the house, and seek diligently till she find it? ⁹ And when she hath found it, she calleth her friends and her neighbours together, saying, Rejoice with me; for I have found the piece which I had lost. ¹⁰ Likewise, I say unto you, there is joy in the presence of the angels of God over one sinner that repenteth."

Copper

A Call to Battle: 1 Cor. 14:8 (KJV): "For if the trumpet give an uncertain sound, who shall prepare himself to the battle?"

Gray

Glory and Power of God: Rev. 15:8 (KJV): "And the temple was filled with smoke from the glory of God, and from his power; and no man was able to enter into the temple."

The smoke of the incense of the saints' prayers: Rev. 8:4 (KJV) "And the smoke of the incense, which came with the prayers of the saints, ascended up before God out of the angel's hand."

Royal Blue

Royalty: Esther 8:15 (NASB): "Then Mordecai went out from the presence of the king in royal robes of blue and white."

Aqua Blue

Blessing: Ezek. 34:26–27a (NIV): "[26] I will make them and the places surrounding my hill a blessing. I will send down showers in season; there will be showers of blessing. [27] The trees will yield their fruit and the ground will yield its crops."

Sapphire/Sky Blue

Heaven: Ex. 24:9, 10 (NIV): "[9] Moses and Aaron, Nadab and Abihu, and the seventy elders of Israel went up [10] and saw the God of Israel. Under his feet was something like a pavement made of sapphire, clear as the sky itself."

Throne of God: Ezek. 1:26 (NIV): "Above the expanse over their heads was what looked like a throne of sapphire, and high above on the throne was a figure like that of a man."

Orange

Consuming Fire: Deut. 4:24 (NIV): "For the LORD your God is a consuming fire, a jealous God."

Judgment, Wrath, Vengeance: 2 Thes. 1:6–7 (NIV): "[6] God is just: He will pay back trouble to those who trouble you [7]and give relief to you who are troubled, and to us as well. This will happen when the Lord Jesus is revealed from heaven in blazing fire with his powerful angels."

Holy Spirit: Acts 2:3–4 (NIV): "[3] They saw what seemed to be tongues of fire that separated and came to rest on each of them. [4] All of them were filled with the Holy Spirit and began to speak in other tongues as the Spirit enabled them."

Black/Darkness (as pertains to God)

God's Surroundings, Covering: 2 Sam. 22:12 (NIV): "He made darkness his canopy around him—the dark rain clouds of the sky"; Ex. 20:21 (NIV): "The people remained at a distance, while Moses approached the thick darkness where God was"; 1 Kings 8:12 (NIV): "Then Solomon said, 'The LORD has said that he would dwell in a dark cloud.'"

Power of God to Destroy: Jos. 24:7 (NIV): "But they cried to the LORD for help, and he put darkness between you and the Egyptians; he brought the sea over them and covered them. You saw with your own eyes what I did to the Egyptians."

Flag colors can also be symbolic of the worship or praise that we are giving God.

Brown (Dust)

Worshiping, Confession: Neh. 9:1–3 (NIV): "[1] On the twenty-fourth day of the same month, the Israelites gathered together, fasting and wearing sackcloth and having dust on their heads. [2] Those of Israelite descent had separated themselves from all foreigners. They stood in their places and confessed their sins and the wickedness of their fathers. [3] They stood where they were and read from the Book of the Law of the LORD their God for a quarter of the day, and spent another quarter in confession and in worshiping the LORD their God."

Color of a lion (light brown)

Praise: Gen. 29:35 (NIV): "She conceived again, and when she gave birth to a son she said, 'This time I will praise the LORD.' So she named him Judah. " Gen. 49:9 (NIV) "You are a lion's cub, Judah."

The above list is not all-inclusive. Other representations and colors can be found in Scripture. I encourage you to find them for yourself. There are no hard and fast rules about what colors to use. I believe what is important is that your heart is clean and that your ministry is a genuine expression of yourself to God, no matter what flag color you use.

The flags make a beautiful display of color and are impressive to see. However, seeing their beauty alone is not a reason to use them. Raised flags show we are identifying with and belong to Jesus as the Spirit of the Lord in Isaiah 59:19, the Captain of the Lord's Host in Joshua 5:14, My Banner in Exodus 17:15, and Faithful and True in Revelation 19:14. Our Jesus is a warrior. He is Jehovah-Tsebaoth, the Lord of Battles. We stand ready for warfare in the supernatural.

5. A Supernatural Operation

The best way to help you understand what I mean by a supernatural operation is to describe one that happened to me, that is, one that the Lord allowed me to see. Afterward I will tell you how this is relevant to the flags.

I went to the altar at church in Germany one Sunday night for prayer in 1992. I wanted more of Jesus. I earnestly prayed for more of Him and expected to receive more of Him. Under the power of the Holy Spirit, I danced uncontrollably—not by my will—for what seemed like forever, nonstop. This dance continued while the pastor preached the sermon. I stopped after the benediction and went totally limp and spent onto the floor. I didn't have enough strength to sit up in the pew alone. When I gradually gained my strength, I was not the same. As I walked, I could not feel the floor under my feet. The second hand on the clock looked like it was moving in slow motion. Every second seemed to be alive. Then I noticed two people talking. One person spoke. As she spoke, a stream of water flowed from her mouth toward him. (John 7:38 NIV: "Whoever believes in me, as the Scripture has said, streams of living water will flow from within him." [39]By this he meant the Holy Spirit.)

As he spoke to her, a stream of water flowed from him to her. I looked around the sanctuary. Only a few people had remained. I looked wide-eyed at another lady who spoke with the same stream of water flowing from her mouth. I could see these streams of water going back and forth between people as they talked! I am convinced this stream of water is love. (Romans 5:5 NIV: "God has poured out his love into our hearts by the Holy Spirit, whom he has given us.") Love comes from God to us and from us to others. I believe words spoken in love have substance and are visible in the supernatural. That love is a translucent stream of water, which flows like a river from one person's mouth onto the person spoken to. It is beautiful, peaceful, gentle, and soothing. I am telling you this because it is evidence of an operation in the supernatural. God said, "Whoever believes in me, streams of living water will flow from within him." That's one supernatural operation. When praising, worshiping, and praying with the flags, another supernatural operation occurs.

I am convinced that warfare on our behalf happens in the supernatural or spirit realm when we use flags with prayer, because Ephesians 6:11–18 (KJV) tells us to pray when the enemy comes, Jeremiah 50:2 tells us to raise a flag and say the enemy is taken, and Isaiah 59:19 KJV tells us the Spirit of the Lord will make the enemy flee or vanish.

The Spirit of the Lord Will Make the Enemy Flee

The Spirit of the Lord will make the enemy flee. Sin and evil are enemies of the Lord. Sin was very prevalent during old testament times. Isaiah 59: 12-16 (The Message) says

> 12-15Our wrongdoings pile up before you, God, our sins stand up and accuse us. Our wrongdoings stare us down; we know in detail what we've done: Mocking and denying God, not following our God, Spreading false rumors, inciting sedition, pregnant with lies, muttering malice. Justice is beaten back, Righteousness is banished to the sidelines, Truth staggers down the street, Honesty is nowhere to be found, Good is missing in action.

Anyone renouncing evil is beaten and robbed. [15-16]God looked and saw evil looming on the horizon— so much evil and no sign of Justice. He couldn't believe what he saw: not a soul around to correct this awful situation.

The Spirit of the Lord responded to the presence of His enemy, evil. This is the supernatural operation that the Lord did then and does today against evil: The Spirit of the Lord puts on His battle armor. Isaiah 59:16-17 (KJV) says,

> therefore his arm brought salvation unto him; and his righteousness, it sustained him. [17]For he put on righteousness as a breastplate, and an helmet of salvation upon his head; and he put on the garments of vengeance for clothing, and was clad with zeal as a cloak.

Why did He put on His armor? He was preparing to do battle against His enemies because He is a God of vengeance. After He puts on His armor, what does He then do? He repays his enemies for what they have done with fury. Isaiah 59:18 (KJV) says,

> According to their deeds, accordingly he will repay fury to his adversaries, recompense to his enemies; to the islands he will repay recompense.

Exactly how does God repay His enemies? The spirit of the Lord repays his enemies by lifting up a standard against them. The *Hebrew Chaldee Dictionary* (5127) says "shall lift up a standard" comes from the root word "nuwc" which means *to vanish away, make to flee away, put to flight.*

> When the enemy shall come in like a flood, <u>the Spirit of the LORD shall lift up a standard against him</u> (Isaiah 59:19b KJV).

This is a supernatural operation. What does that mean to us today? When looking in the New Testament in Ephesians 6, we are told that we wrestle against spiritual wickedness in high places. There was spiritual wickedness then. There is spiritual wickedness today. Although time has moved through centuries, evil is nothing new and still plagues the Earth as much as it did then. Because we have enemies today, we should not fear, because the Lord our God will protect us. Numbers 10:9 KJV reminds us that: "ye shall be remembered before the LORD your God, and ye shall be saved from your enemies."

For our protection, we are told to put on (spiritual) armor. This means we must use the supernatural weapons God has available to us, e.g., truth, righteousness, peace, faith, salvation, and the Word of God, to come against the evil of this world. Ephesians 6:13–17 (KJV) says:

> [13] Wherefore take unto you the whole armor of God that ye may be able to withstand in the evil day, and having done all, to stand. [14] Stand therefore, having your loins girt about with truth, and having on the breastplate of righteousness; [15] And your feet shod with the preparation of the gospel of peace; [16] Above all, taking the shield of faith, wherewith ye shall be able to quench all the fiery darts of the wicked. [17] And take the helmet of salvation, and the sword of the Spirit, which is the word of God.

The full armor is described in Isaiah 59:17. God did not put on truth, peace, and the Word. He *is* the truth, peace, and the Word. And He lifted a flag. We were told to put on the whole armor of God except for God's "garments of vengeance for clothing, and zeal as a cloak."

This is said because Romans 12:19 (KJV) states: "Dearly beloved, avenge not yourselves, but rather give place unto wrath: for it is written, Vengeance is mine; I will repay, saith the Lord." And because 2 Chronicles 20:15b (KJV) says: "for the battle is not yours, but God's."

God allowed Joshua to see into the supernatural realm. The Lord fought a battle for the Israelites because the battle was His and not theirs. The Lord is the commander of the army of the Lord in Joshua 5:9–15 (KJV). Also, Jesus is the Captain of the Lord's Host. He is our Captain.

> [9]And the LORD said unto Joshua, This day have I rolled away the reproach of Egypt from off you. Wherefore the name of the place is called Gilgal unto this day. [10]And the children of Israel encamped in Gilgal, and kept the passover on the fourteenth day of the month at even in the plains of Jericho.... [13]And it came to pass, when Joshua was by Jericho, that he lifted up his eyes and looked, and, behold, there stood a man over against him with his sword drawn in his hand: and Joshua went unto him, and said unto him, Art thou for us, or for our adversaries? [14]And he said, Nay; but as captain of the host of the LORD am I now come. And Joshua fell on his face to the earth, and did worship, and said unto him, What saith my Lord unto his servant? [15]And the captain of the LORD's host said unto Joshua, Loose thy shoe from off thy foot; for the place whereon thou standest is holy. And Joshua did so.

The Captain of the Lord's host goes ahead of us and fights the battle. Again 2 Chronicles 20:15 (KJV) says "the battle is not yours, but God's." Another instance where the Lord does battle in the supernatural is described in Isaiah 31:5–9 (NIV). We see that by the mere sight of the battle standard (flag) the enemy will panic:

> [5] Like birds hovering overhead, the LORD Almighty will shield Jerusalem; he will shield it and deliver it, he will "pass over" it and will rescue it. [6] Return to him

you have so greatly revolted against, O Israelites. [7] For in that day every one of you will reject the idols of silver and gold your sinful hands have made. [8] Assyria will fall by a sword that is not of man; a sword, not of mortals, will devour them. They will flee before the sword and their young men will be put to forced labor. [9] Their stronghold will fall because of terror; at sight of the battle standard their commanders will panic, declares the LORD, whose fire is in Zion, whose furnace is in Jerusalem.

These are supernatural operations. The operation that is being carried out is warfare. That is, warfare in the supernatural realm. So, why use the flag with praise or worship in a church or home? We can use the flag with praise and worship for warfare, more specifically, supernatural warfare. We engage in supernatural warfare when we pray.

6. Prayer

Warfare on people's behalf happens in the supernatural realm against our enemies when the flag bearer prays while waving the flags. Today's enemies are disease, poverty, and broken families just to name a few.

Pray When The Enemy Comes

In general, the Bible makes it plain in the New Testament that all people are to pray. Ephesians 6:18 (KJV) says: "Praying always with all prayer and supplication in the Spirit, and watching thereunto with all perseverance and supplication for all saints."

Specifically, for the one who raises the flags (the flag bearer), you are to declare and say "the enemy is taken". Raise a flag and speak. Claim your enemy is beaten. For example, the Babylonians were the Israelites' enemies. Bel was the deity or god of the Babylonians and Merodach was one of their kings. Jeremiah 50:2–3 (KJV) says:

> ² Declare ye among the nations and publish [*make noise, declare*], and set up [*lift up or raise*] a standard; publish, and conceal not: say, Babylon is taken, Bel is put to shame, Merodach is dismayed; her images are put to shame, her idols are dismayed. ³ For out of the north there cometh up a nation against her, which shall make

her land desolate, and none shall dwell therein: they are fled, they are gone, both man and beast. [Phrases in italics are from the *Hebrew and Chaldee Dictionary* items 8085 and 5375, respectively.]

Flag bearers, raise a banner and then make a battle cry. From the example in Isaiah 13:1–5 (The Message), open your mouth. The standard was risen first, and then the battle cry was given.

Isaiah 13:1–5 (The Message) says:

> [1] The Message on Babylon. Isaiah son of Amoz saw it:
> [2-3] "Run up a flag on an open hill. Yell loud. Get their attention. Wave them into formation. Direct them to the nerve center of power. I've taken charge of my special forces, called up my crack troops. They're bursting with pride and passion to carry out my angry judgment."
> [4-5] Thunder rolls off the mountains like a mob huge and noisy—Thunder of kingdoms in an uproar, nations assembling for war. God-of-the-Angel-Armies is calling his army into battle formation. They come from far-off countries, they pour in across the horizon. It's God on the move with the weapons of his wrath, ready to destroy the whole country.

Flag bearers have faith. Depend on God when he says in Mark 11:22–24 (KJV):

> [22] And Jesus answering saith unto them, Have faith in God. [23] For verily I say unto you, That whosoever shall say unto this mountain, Be thou removed, and be thou cast into the sea; and shall not doubt in his heart, but shall believe that those things which he saith shall come to pass; he shall have whatsoever he saith. [24] Therefore I say unto you, What things soever ye desire, when ye

pray, believe that ye receive them, and ye shall have them.

Will God find faith in you? Will God find faith in your church or home because of you? Will God find you using your faith as you pray for others while you use the flags on behalf of others? Luke 18:8 says, "when the Son of Man comes, will he find faith on the earth?"

God will hear you when you call out to Him in prayer while you wave your flags. You will have certain victory. You can count on it. Psalm 20:4–9 (KJV) says:

> ⁴ Grant thee according to thine own heart, and fulfil all thy counsel. ⁵ We will rejoice in thy salvation, and in the name of our God we will set up our banners [*raise a flag*]: the LORD fulfill all thy petitions. ⁶ Now know I that the LORD saveth his anointed; he will hear him from his holy heaven with the saving strength of his right hand. ⁷ Some trust in chariots, and some in horses: but we will remember the name of the LORD our God. ⁸ They are brought down and fallen: but we are risen, and stand upright. ⁹ Save, LORD: let the king hear us when we call. (Raise a flag comes from the *Hebrew and Chaldee Dictionary* number 1713.)

This is what I have come to understand: The Lord, the commander of the Lord's army, the Lord of Hosts, the Lord of Battles, Jehovah-Tsebaoth, puts on his armor and raises a flag against the enemy. We flag bearers are intercessors who pray for others, as told in Ephesians 6:18. "Men ought always to pray" (Luke 18:1). We flag bearers are some of the intercessors of the land now, whereas in Isaiah 59:16–19 (KJV), "there was no intercessor":

> ¹⁶ And he saw that there was no man, and wondered that there was no intercessor: therefore his arm

brought salvation unto him; and his righteousness, it sustained him. [17] For he put on righteousness as a breastplate, and an helmet of salvation upon his head; and he put on the garments of vengeance for clothing, and was clad with zeal as a cloak. [18] According to their deeds, accordingly he will repay, fury to his adversaries, recompense to his enemies; to the islands he will repay recompense. [19] So shall they fear the name of the LORD from the west, and his glory from the rising of the sun. When the enemy shall come in like a flood, the Spirit of the LORD shall lift up a standard against him.

When we pray sincerely in faith with our armor on while raising our flags that have been consecrated to the Lord, we are identifying with Him. We do what He does (that is, put on armor and raise a flag). We are signaling to Him that we are with Him and ready to move out. We move out in prayer. He moves out to do battle in the spirit realm. Remember, vengeance is His, not ours.

When we pray for help, the Lord of Hosts or commander of the Lord's army steps in and fights our battles to win victories in our lives and in the lives of those we pray for.

When you raise your flags, use music. Isaiah 30:30–32 (NIV) says:

[30] The LORD will cause men to hear his majestic voice and will make them see his arm coming down with raging anger and consuming fire, with cloudburst, thunderstorm and hail. [31] The voice of the LORD will shatter Assyria; with his scepter he will strike them down. [32] Every stroke the LORD lays on them with his punishing rod will be to the music of tambourines

and harps, as he fights them in battle with the blows
of his arm.

Open your mouth. Praise God. Praise Him again. And praise Him.
In prayer, tell God that according to His Word, He is a provider, healer,
deliverer, etc. Ask Him in Jesus' name to come and provide, heal,
deliver, etc. In faith, declare your enemy is defeated in Jesus' name. We
can ask God to tell us what to pray for.

*How Biblical Uses of Banners Translate into Today's Use of Flags in the
Body of Christ*

So far in your reading, from the chapter entitled The Flag Bearer,
we have seen flags that have been consecrated. From the chapter entitled
Love, the flag bearer examines or assesses him- or herself. From the
chapter entitled The Flag Bearer, we have the flag bearer making him-
or herself clean before picking up the flags, by confessing his or her
sin and asking God for forgiveness. We see that flag colors can be
associated with different attributes of God. We also see that flag bearers
are engaged in spiritual warfare through prayer.

So how do we put this to practical use today? We have reached a
point in this book where the flag bearer is ready to pick up the flags
and use them. Psalm 20:5 says, "We will rejoice in thy salvation, and
in the name of our God we will set up our banners: the LORD fulfill
all thy petitions." What requests are you making to God on behalf of
the congregation, your family, yourself, and others? Perhaps healing is
one petition. One of the representations of green could be health or that
which promotes healing. So we may want to use a green flag while we
are asking God for healing. Or use a purple flag, which could represent
God's majesty, royalty, authority, and kingship. With all authority, God
can do anything.

The flag bearer picks up the consecrated flags under the direction
of the Holy Spirit. He or she is carrying one flag in each hand. This is

an example of a prayer for healing in doing spiritual warfare with the flags. This sample prayer has three basic sections: humble yourself, tell the Holy Spirit how wonderful you think He is, and let Him know what you need help with. In humbling yourself, you are letting the Holy Spirit know that you know your position is low compared to Him. In telling the Holy Spirit how wonderful you think He is, you are letting Him know your heart toward Him, that you know who He is, and that you adore Him for who He is. In telling Him what you need, you are acknowledging to Him that based on his Word or Scripture, you depend on Him. You are letting Him know that you have some enemies that you need Him to defeat. This can be done (without lip movement) while the flag bearer is dancing and waving flags to the rhythm of praise or worship music. This can be done while at home or in front of a church congregation or any other place where ministry is occurring. In the following example, the flag bearer could use green flags (symbolic of healing) with the praise song, "Lord, You're Mighty" from the album *Resting on His Promise* by JJ Hairston & Youthful Praise:

> *Humble yourself:* I, a lowly sinner saved by your grace, come to you. I come before you naked *(alone and without being covered by your presence).* Come to me, Father. Please cover me with your anointing. Hide me. May I ascend the hill of the Lord? May I stand in your holy place? Thank you, God, for your righteousness. Without you I am nothing. My best deeds are like filthy rags. I depend on you. You are the vine and I am a branch. For that I say thank you.

> *Tell the Holy Spirit how wonderful you think He is and that you welcome His presence*: I welcome you here, Holy Spirit, into this place. Lead me, Lord. I don't

want to go ahead of you. I adore you, my mighty God. You are majestic in all the Earth! How excellent is your name! You are Ruler, King of Kings! There is none like you. None can compare to you, O mighty God. I thank you, God, that you are Jehovah, my Healer. I thank you, God, for the stripes by which your people are healed.

Tell Him what you need and make your request based on Scripture: God, we've got some people here today who need your healing power. I know you have the power to overcome disease. Your Word tells me you healed a blind man, a leper, and a woman with an issue of blood. I ask you to show yourself. I ask you to bring healing today, in the name of Jesus. You told me to speak to the mountain. I say, cancer, be gone in Jesus's name! All manner of mental, emotional, and physical disease be gone, in Jesus's name! You told me in Jeremiah 50 to raise a flag and say Babylon is taken. I say all our enemies are taken, in Jesus' name! Replace disease with healing in the name of Jesus!

Praying with Flags for Victory Is Rooted in Psalm 20

Flags can be used while praying for victory on behalf of those who are oppressed, downtrodden, brokenhearted, and sick because of Psalm 20:5–9 (KJV).

> [5]We will rejoice in thy salvation, and in the name of our God we will set up our banners: the LORD fulfill all thy petitions. [6]Now know I that the LORD saveth his anointed; he will hear him from his holy heaven with

the saving strength of his right hand. ⁷Some trust in chariots, and some in horses: but we will remember the name of the LORD our God. ⁸They are brought down and fallen: but we are risen, and stand upright. ⁹Save, LORD: let the king hear us when we call.

We can pray for healing because we have a King who hears us when we call. The flag bearer may want to declare God is King and has all authority, while using a purple flag.

One Sunday, I was entrusted to minister with the flags before the services began at my church, in order to help set the atmosphere to receive the Word of God from my pastor. While I was waving my tie-dyed purple silk flag, I was talking to God, telling Him how majestic He is and how all authority in heaven and on Earth has been given to Him (Matt. 28:18). Among other things, I told Him that He has authority over sickness. I asked Him to take authority over sickness and to remove it in the name of Jesus. A few days later, a young lady who had been in the congregation came to me. She shared how she had been healed from a severe debilitating migraine headache. In faith, she had been praying for healing. She had a vision. In her vision, an angel came to her and stroked her face three times. On the third stroke, the migraine headache left. The young lady said the angel was wearing a garment made of a fabric and color just like the purple tie-dyed silk flag I used. I was just so amazed. To God be the glory.

Declaring Victory and Staking Claim on Territory with Flags Is Rooted in Jeremiah 50

We can declare victory and stake a claim on territory. We can declare victory over disease, to be replaced with a territory of healing; brokenness replaced by wholeness; anxiety replaced by peace; lack replaced by plenty; independence from God replaced by trust and dependence upon God; lies replaced by truth; fear replaced by faith; and so on. Jeremiah 50:2–3 (KJV) says:

> ² Declare ye among the nations, and publish, and set up a standard; publish, and conceal not: say, Babylon is taken, Bel is confounded, Merodach is broken in pieces; her idols are confounded, her images are broken in pieces. ³ For out of the north there cometh up a nation against her, which shall make her land desolate, and none shall dwell therein: they shall remove, they shall depart, both man and beast.

I got in my bed about 8:30 on a Saturday night on August 22, 2009 with no intention of ministering to the song "I Give Myself Away" by William McDowell. I began to feel compelled by the Holy Spirit to get up from my bed to create a choreography with the flags in order to minister that song; that is, minister that song the next morning, Sunday the 23rd. Even more compelling was to walk up and down the center aisle of my church's sanctuary waving a giant-sized purple flag over the heads of the people who sat to the right and left of the aisle. That purple flag had a drawing of a gold king's crown on it. By 9:30 p.m., I had the choreography where I would use two large hand flags during the first half of the song and one giant-sized purple king crown flag during the remainder of the song. After getting permission from my dance leader, I ministered this as the praise team sang at three services that Sunday (7:30, 9:00, and 11:15 a.m.). During the first two services, I waved the king crown flag high above the people's heads. While waving that flag, I prayed. I told God He is majestic. King. He has authority over disease. I asked Him to heal. I said, "Diseases be gone in the name of Jesus." I did the same thing at the 11:15 service. Something different happened during that service with the king crown flag. As I was waving the flag high above the people's heads as they were standing, the flag lowered itself on its own. The Holy Spirit took control of the flag. The flag nearly touched people's heads as it circled the right side of the sanctuary. My bishop got on one knee in front of the congregation and viewed under the flag as it moved over the heads of the people. My bishop stood up. He called a woman to come to the front of the sanctuary. She did as asked. He said, in effect, Healing was in the sanctuary right now. He prayed for God to heal her body from a chronic leukemia. After medical treatments, the woman is healed in the name Jesus.

I believe the Holy Spirit as Jehovah Tsebaoth brought healing to the sanctuary during that service. I also believe Jehovah Tsebaoth caused the enemy to flee. The flag was *published* and *not concealed* that morning. On October 25, 2011 I watched a video of what happened during that service on Sunday, August 23, 2009. After watching the video, I was reminded that the bishop and his wife had been walking in faith since Wednesday August 19, 2009 for God to show up and do something on that Sunday. During their fasting period, God had spoken that He was going to move that Sunday. The bishop did not know which of the three services that would happen. It happened during that third service in which the Holy Spirit took control of the flag. I believe God was at work to answer the prayers of all the saints who had been praying for healing. God uses our faith and the flags. *Babylon* (chronic leukemia) *was taken. God is faithful to His* Word. God will do what He says He will do.

Showing Allegiance to God with Flags Is Rooted in Numbers 2:1–34 (NIV)

The different tribes of Israel used standards and banners to show the tribe to which they belonged. They also followed that particular standard and banner when they broke camp and set out to march across the desert. The flag bearer can raise a consecrated flag to show that he or she and the assembled congregation belong to, show allegiance to, and follow God, who has the particular attribute that the flag represents.

Using Flags to Rally the Congregation Is Rooted in Isaiah 11:6–16 (The Message).

The flag bearer indicates the point where the congregation and heavenly forces are to meet. In the sanctuary. In the home.

Using Flags to Signal the Congregation Is Rooted in Isaiah 5:25–30 (The Message).

The flag bearer sends the congregation and the heavenly forces signals. The signals are those attributes that are represented by the flags. With a purple flag, the signals could be Majesty. Authority. King.

Using Flags to Herald an Event is Rooted in Isaiah 18:1–7 (The Message).

The flag bearer is letting the congregation and the heavenly forces know that something is about to happen. God is about to manifest Himself.

The flag bearers can use the flags before a worship service at church to declare allegiance to God, who is our Banner or the one we follow. We can use the flags to rally and signal the troops (believers in the congregation and forces in the spirit realm) that we are about to engage in spiritual warfare. We are calling on Jesus as the Spirit of the Lord, Jehovah-Tsebaoth, to put our enemy to flight (Isaiah 59:19). Sometimes I would stand before the congregation during the invocation with two flags raised, one in each hand. I just stand there with these flags raised high, and I pray with my lips barely moving. I tell God that all of us in church this day at this time belong to Him. I call on the Lord of Battles, the Spirit of the Lord to come to us.

Using Flags to Bestow Honor to God Is Rooted in Exodus 17:9–16 (KJV).

Moses erected an altar to honor God for the victory God won against the Amalekites. Moses called that altar the Lord Is My Banner. By definition, a standard is something conspicuous and easily seen; a symbol. The altar was conspicuous and easily seen and a symbol to memorialize Jehovah. Hence, it was referred to as a banner. Flag bearers use them to give great honor to God.

Hopefully, I have brought you to a point where you understand why a flag bearer uses flags during praise and worship in the church. They enhance the worship service at the church. They may also enhance our worship at home. They can be used as a tool by God to bring people healing under the power of the Holy Spirit.

Questions Answered after the Search

My personal search for understanding the meaning and scriptural basis of flags began in 2003, when the Holy Spirit took control of the streamer I was holding while praise dancing and praying to God at church. (The streamer is a type of flag instrument.) My initial question in 2003 had been why did the Holy Spirit take control of my streamer? The answer is, it belongs to Him. It is for Him to use. He is the Spirit of the Lord and Jehovah-Tsebaoth. "When the enemy shall come in like a flood, the Spirit of the Lord shall lift up a standard against him" (Isa. 59:19 KJV). He raises a flag against the enemy. What flag? I believe it is my flag, your flag, and our flags. This seven-year journey has brought me to a place where I also understand why I use flags and to understand that warfare on people's behalf happens in the spiritual realm. I learned the answer to another question, which had simply been why do we use flags in church? The simple answer is because that is God's will. "We will rejoice in thy salvation, and in the name of our God we will set up our banners [*raise a flag*]: the LORD fulfill all thy petitions," says Psalm 20:5.

Flag bearers, when the Holy Spirit comes, He may take control of the flags. The flags belong to Him. Be amazed. I do hope that every flag bearer gets used for this purpose. May God bless you.

7. Flag Movements
and A Practical Exercise

There are basically two types of movements: movements that are choreographed by you and movements that are choreographed by the Holy Spirit. You may begin with movements that are choreographed by you, and a shift may occur when the Holy Spirit takes over the moves.

Your choreography may be spontaneous or rehearsed techniques made into a dance. No matter what the moves are, always pray.

Home is a good place to start using the flags with the Lord. This is where you can learn how to become comfortable with the flags in praise and worship. If you have never used a flag, you may want to practice handling a pair of medium-sized hybrid or twirling flags (see chapter on Flag Construction), one in each hand until you become comfortable with waving them. Resources where you may purchase flags or banners are included at the end of the book.

It's a good idea to warm up your shoulders and arms by stretching those muscles before using the flags. This may help prevent injury. Also stretch the muscles after using the flags to help reduce soreness.

Listed below are some basic movements, moves, or techniques for you. Other moves may be given to you by the Holy Spirit. As a start, you can begin to move your flags with these movements or whatever the

Holy Spirit leads you to do. Place one flag in each hand. Repeat each movement until you can flow smoothly and easily with them.

Figure 1: Extend both flags to the left. Bring both flags overhead and then down to the right side of your body, creating an arch. Move flags with arms extended from the right, overhead, and then to the left side of your body.

Reverse/change direction

Figure 2: Raise the flags, arms fully extended above your shoulders. Slowly turn your body in a circle. Change direction so that you don't become dizzy.

Repeat Steps 2 & 3

Figure 3: Raise flags overhead. Bring the right flag down below waist level to the left. Bring the left flag down to the right and return the right hand to overhead position.. While one hand is down, the other should be up. Continue to alternate the pattern where one hand is up the other is down.

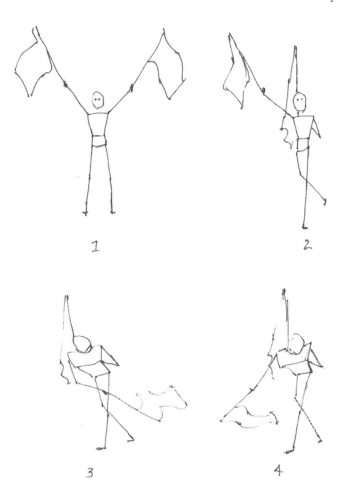

Figure 4: Raise both flags overhead. Place the left flag behind your back and extend your right leg behind you. Bring the right flag down in a wide arch to the left below knee level, then swing it to your right. As you swing the flag to the right, bow your head.

Figure 5: Use one flag at a time. Begin with flag in your right hand. Fully extend your right arm to your right. Imagine a large "8" in front of you that is lying horizontal. Use the flag to create this 8 pattern. Use the flag in the left hand. Extend your left arm to your left. Use both flags.

Create movements of your own. Also, a DVD by Pastor Lynn Hayden entitled Perfume of Fire showing other flag movements is available from Dancing for Him Ministries (see Resources).

Now that you are familiar with how the movements feel and you see how you control their movement, I encourage you to worship with the flags along with music. Move your flags to the beat of the music, using any of the movements given you. Create your own patterns. Remember to consecrate your flags before you use them. Select a flag color based on the attribute you will be praying about God as you use the flags. Examine yourself, especially in comparison to 1 Corinthians 13, the love chapter.

Say a prayer to confess known sin in your life. Ask for forgiveness. (Let God know that you know you are lower than Him; that is, humble yourself before Him. You can follow the sample prayer offered in the chapter on prayer as a guide, especially paragraphs one and two. Substitute your own words where appropriate.) Ask the Holy Spirit to guide your movements. I suggest you start by playing one of your favorite worship songs, or "Redeemer" from the album *Redeemer: The Best of Nicole C. Mullen.* Think about what the song is saying about our Lord. As you listen to the song, focus on the words. What do the words remind you or tell you about the Lord? Let the words you hear jar your memory of all the attributes you know about our Lord from Scripture or experience. Quote out loud or paraphrase those Scriptures to the Lord while you move with the flags to the beat of the music. (Rosemary Jensen[5] singled out many Bible verses that exemplify or explain God's attributes in *Praying the Attributes of God.* Lester Sumrall[6] described God's nature by His many names as Jehovah in *The Names of God.* In addition to the Bible, Ms. Jensen's and Mr. Sumrall's books are handy references for this purpose.) Just move the flags to the beat of the music. Focus on what you are thinking about and telling our God. This is not a recipe, but a style that I am accustomed to. You may already have your own way of entering worship. You talk to God the way you do in order to enter intimate worship with Him. (When ministering to a

---

5   Rosemary Jensen, *Praying the Attributes of God.* Kregel Publications, 2002, ISBN 0–8254–2942-0.
6   Lester Sumrall, *The Names of God.* Whitaker House Publisher, 1982, ISBN –13: 978-0–88368–779–6.

congregation, keep your lips still as you talk to Him or pray. To the people who are watching you, the lip movement can distract from your flag ministry.)

The more you become accustomed to the flags, the more they will become an extension of you. You won't think about them. Your attention and focus will be on your heartfelt worship to our Lord. Expect the Holy Spirit to use you.

8. Flag Construction

The flag has a pole, fabric, and sometimes a sleeve, ball or end cap. Four aspects of a flag's construction are its style, size, shape, and weight. These qualities can dictate how and when to use particular flags. There is nothing scriptural about this. It's a matter of practicality and presentation.

Style

The style of flag pertains to how the fabric moves around its pole. The fabric can either swivel freely around the pole because it is not attached to the pole or it cannot swivel freely because it is attached to the pole. The three basic styles of flags are twirling, non-twirling, and hybrid. The style determines the variety of movements the flag bearer can or cannot make while using the flags.

	Type of Pole	Sleeve	Fabric Attached to	Weight	Pros	Cons
Twirling Flag	Metal; Fiber glass; Wood; Plastic	Yes	Sleeve	Slightly heavier by ounces	Flag swivels freely around pole	Flag is slightly heavier than other style flags

Non-twirling flag	Wood; Fiber glass; Plastic	No	Pole	Lighter by ounces	The flag is a lighter weight. Less tiring.	The fabric does not swivel freely around the pole
Hybrid flag	Wood; Fiber glass; Plastic	No	Nothing; it slips over the pole	Lighter by ounces	Fabric swivels freely around the pole; the flag is lighter in weight	

Twirling (or twirl) flags have poles or shafts that have sleeves (swivel tubes) over them. The flag's fabric is then attached to the sleeves typically with Velcro. To aid in handling, a ball-shaped handle is placed at the end of the pole. By design the fabric of the twirling flag swivels freely around the pole or shaft without wrapping itself around the pole. I have found the twirling flag allows flag bearers to create a larger variety of movements compared to the non-twirling flag.

Non-twirling flags use a pole without a sleeve. The flag's fabric is attached directly to the pole. They may or may not have a cap at the end of the handle. The fabric of the non-twirling flag does not swivel freely around the pole. This limits the choices of flag movements the flag bearer can make. This style may be appropriate for the choreography you use.

A hybrid of the twirling and non-twirling flags has the advantages of both and none of the disadvantages of either. It's made of a pole (rod) and fabric. Some do have end caps. The flag's fabric is not attached to the pole. The pole sleeve or swivel tube is part of the fabric itself in that a very stiff interfacing is used for a casing. This allows the fabric to swivel freely around the pole. This style too allows the flag bearer to create a large variety of flag movements. It doesn't have the added ounces of the twirling flag because it is made from fewer parts.

Size

Flags come in different sizes. The appropriate size used is determined by the amount of space in which it will be used and the person's size. Children will typically use a small flag, whereas an adult will use a larger flag. You may want to use medium flags in crowded, tight spaces and larger flags in roomier spaces. You may want to use a medium flag in your home. The smaller the flag, the easier it is to use for very fast movements. The twirl flag is great for fast movements. Flags come in sizes small (about 16" x 19"), medium (20" x 25"), large (26" x 30"), extra large (33" x 40") and even larger. Some gigantic flag sizes are appropriate for stadiums or rooms with tall ceilings. Size dimensions can vary depending upon who makes the flags.

Shape

What about the flag's shape? The different shapes can be attractive and pretty to see. And they can create different effects while in motion. Some common shapes are square, rectangular, half-circle, one-quarter circle, and swallow tail.

Weight

The weight of the flags is another difference. The hybrid and non-twirling flags are made of a pole, fabric and sometimes an end cap. Typically the twirling flag can be a few ounces heavier than these. This is due to the amount of material that is used to make the twirling flag, i.e., the pole or shaft, the sleeve, the ball and the fabric. That could mean you have to use a little more arm strength to wave them around. In spite of this, this is a great style of flag to use. Many flag bearers appreciate the extra ounces. Most flag poles or shafts are made of wood, plastic, fiber glass or metal. Wood (or dowel) is the lighter weight material where metal is the heaviest.

Fabrics come in different weights, from light to medium to heavy. With less weight, the flag is more likely to float on the air a few seconds after the hand has stopped moving the flag. For this reason, the lighter-weight flags are best suited for movements that are very soft, long, and slow. The medium to heavier weights are more suited for moderate to fast movements. However, they can also be used for slower movements. The heavier the fabric, the louder the noise it makes as it ruffles through the air. The heavier the fabric, the more tired it will make the arms.

The choices of flags for the flag bearer to use in a church setting are too numerous to describe here. I suggest you consider the tempo of the music, the weight of the fabric, the style of the flag and the amount of space in which you will be waving the flags. You should use the appropriate size flag for the allowed space so that you avoid hitting objects and people. People expect you to control your flags. Do not expect them to avoid you. If you do hit someone accidently, do apologize right away.

For home use, I do recommend the beginning adult flag bearer use a medium sized hybrid or twirling flag, unless you have a room large enough to accommodate a large flag. I also recommend these fabrics: china silk (polyester), lame, or a medium weight pure silk. All these fabrics are medium weight and work well with slow to moderate movements. These styles and fabrics work well for the tempos of most of your praise and worship songs. The twirl flag works best for the faster tempo songs.

As you become familiar with the flags, you can determine which style, size, shape, and weight are best suited for your use. Also, God can give you specific instructions on what flag or banner to construct or use.

Afterword

God tells us in the Bible to raise the flags. The Holy Spirit intervenes when we use the flags. When the enemy comes in, He will raise that flag against the enemy to bring healing when we pray in the name of Jesus.

I am convinced that warfare on our behalf happens in the spiritual realm when we use the flags and banners with prayer. In addition to prayer and the Holy Spirit, the flag bearer, color, Scripture, love, flag movement, flag construction, and music participate in bringing people healing.

Using flags can be quite an adventure with God. I do hope God uses you in His work. Admit to Him that you don't want to go ahead of Him and that you want to follow Him. Then expect Him to lead you. He may even compel you to join Him. He uses hands in the Earth to hold the flags, to raise the flags. The Holy Spirit can and may control the flags that are in your hands, to bless you and others who may be worshiping.

Resources

SonDanceMinistry.com
Dardenne Prairie, MO
(636) 485-0697

CreationsAnewFlags.com
Newport Richey, FL
(727) 992-3808

WorshipBanners.org
Morehead City, NC
1-877-943-5348

BannersfortheShepherd.com
Boulder, CO
1-800-889-1953

JesusPaintings.com
Sevierville, TN
(865) 908-0075

SilkWorshipFlags.com
Dunedin, FL
(727) 698-6674

ItsAboutWorship.com
Sheffield, AL
(256) 366-9715

Worship-Flags.com
Lancaster, PA
(717) 295-5732

WorshipProducts.com
Deerfield Beach, FL
(561) 394-9214

NewCovenantWorship.com
Plainfield, IL
(815) 230-5332

ILoveWorshipDance.com
Newport, NC
(252) 240-9474

ForHisGlory.com
Klamath Falls, OR
(541) 892-1604

AgapeBanners.com
Houston, TX
(713) 443-2020

RaisedPraise.com
Starkville, MS
(662) 312-8391

EnteringHisGatesFlags.com
West Berlin, NJ

PropheticWorshipBanners.com
Visalia, CA
(559) 901-6285

BannersByRose.com
Grants Pass, OR
(541) 474-9455

Silkhand.com
Largo, FL
(727) 530-3826

Wings2Praise.com
Brandon, FL
(813) 546-1018

DancingForHim.com
Lakeland, FL
DVD: *Perfume of Fire* for Flag Movements/does not sell flags

References

Drummond, Henry (1851–1897). "The Greatest Thing In The World."

Jensen, Rosemary. *Praying the Attributes of God.* Kregel Publications, 2002.

Sumrall, Lester. *The Names of God.* Whitaker House Publisher, 1982.

Unger's Bible Dictionary, Moody Press, copyright 1985.

Notes

Be Thou Exalted

Notes

Notes

Notes

Notes

Printed in Great Britain
by Amazon